Yuletide Favorites for
Ukulele

A Treasury of Fifty Christmas Hymns, Carols & Songs

by Dick Sheridan

INCLUDES
Traditional American & English Carols
Songs from Other Countries
Seasonal & Holiday Tunes
Wassails, Ancient Airs & Dances
~oOo~
Arranged with melody in standard notation,
Easy-to-read tablature,
Chord symbols and diagrams,
Lyrics and comments

ISBN 978-1-57424-286-7
SAN 683-8022

Cover by James Creative Group

Copyright © 2012 CENTERSTREAM Publishing, LLC
P.O. Box 17878 - Anaheim Hills, CA 92817

www.centerstream-usa.com

A DEDICATION
~To my sister Mary~
o0o
With a song in her heart,
especially if it's Irish.

"I heard the bells on Christmas day, their old familiar carols play!"

INTRODUCTION

W hat would Christmas be without music! And what would music be without the ukulele! This humble instrument, so small and seemingly insignificant, has yet made its contribution, and it is far from a meager one. Humble, indeed. Yet so was the birth at Bethlehem, and perhaps in that light it seems particularly appropriate that the ukulele should be enjoined to Christmas and the vast treasury of carols and festive music of this enchanted season.

My link to the ukulele began with a Christmas many years ago. It was a gift, one that I eyed suspiciously and with some regret since I had hoped for a guitar and not a diminutive hourglass instrument with short catgut strings. The song book that came with it was daunting: each melody note had a diagram above it, a crisscross of horizontal and vertical lines representing strings and frets with dots indicating where fingers were to be placed. The challenge of playing was overwhelming, and I soon lost interest. Up on a closet shelf went the ukulele, song book and all.

The following summer, in the throes of childhood boredom, I took down the ukulele and reluctantly re-opened the song book. But this time I discovered that in addition to the note-for-note diagrams *above* the melody there were diagrams *below*, and there were far fewer of them. Several of these other diagrams had more than just one dot. When I place my fingers as indicated and strummed, not just a single note was sounded but a blend of notes. A CHORD! The uke came alive with rich harmony and a gentle voice that was captivating. I was hooked and have been so ever since.

Even before I learned to play the ukulele, my family's household was filled with the sounds of Christmas music. Other than the radio we had no phonograph or recordings -- we had to make our own music. Although I should add that we did have a vintage wind-up Victrola with a scratchy sounding 78 rpm record of Austrian opera diva Ernestine Schumann-Heink singing "Ave Maria" in German. Obviously, more was needed.

So, in an annual ritual, out came a venerable collection of printed Christmas music. There was Hendrik Willem Van Loon's whimsically illustrated book of carols, sheet music for the popular songs of the day, and old hymnals with faded covers and austere presentations of the carols that we normally thought of as gaily spirited and not at all churchy.

Both of my parents could play the piano, and the upright Weber in the living room was never silent for long during the holidays. How often I stood by the side of the piano singing to my mother's accompaniment as she played from the written page. My father could play by ear, and all the popular seasonal songs were his department. Sometimes we played a duet, he providing the melody on the upper keys while I vamped the chords down below. My sister also had an ear for music. With one finger on the keyboard she could pick out melodies, and there were few she didn't know.

There is in my childhood hometown a lovely white church, colonial in style, situated on a hilltop overlooking the trees and rooftops spread out below. At Christmas time carillon bells were broadcast from the tall steeple, and the sound of those bells pulsated over the town in the frosted winter air. How pleasant to step outside the house to listen or to be serenaded while hurrying along the streets bent on happy holiday errands.

In college, just before Christmas vacation, there was an anticipated tradition for the choir to tour the campus, going from building to building, dorm to dorm, singing from mimeographed sheets of carols and holiday songs. How loudly rang those lustily sung choruses of "Deck The Halls" and "Hodie Christus Natus Est." It was an *a capella* choir without instrumental accompaniment. In retrospect, I think the ukulele would have added a nice touch.

Many years later I assembled a small caroling group, eight voices in all. We started rehearsing right after Thanksgiving and worked hard on learning our four parts of harmony. Then with lighted lanterns and ringing hand-bells, we braved wind, snow, and bitter cold to assemble on village doorsteps and surprise the unwary within. A brief stopover at the town tavern provided a well-needed nip of something to numb the senses. How vivid the memory of one of our carolers inverting the handbell she was carrying and petitioning the bartender to "filler up!"

With reflections such as these, and with many years to look back on, my memories are filled with bygone Christmases, musical and otherwise. Perhaps like mine yours bring the sound of carols and bells, choirs and holiday concerts, images of sing-along sleigh rides, street vendors roasting chestnuts, eggnogs, hot buttered rum, candlelight services, Midnight Mass, recitations of "The Night Before Christmas," or a reading of Dylan Thomas' "A Child's Christmas In Wales." Now, for your future memories, as well as for your current enjoyment, I offer you a collection of my favorite carols arranged for the ukulele to add mirth and merriment to your "jolly wassail."

And as I hold my old time-worn Harmony ukulele and run my hand over its mellowed finish, I think of the skilled hands now stilled that crafted it, and a line comes to mind just as suitable for the ukulele's wood as it was for that of an early keyboard instrument on which was engraved:

"In the forest I stood mute and silent. Now in death I sweetly sing."

On the back cover of one of my many folders of instrumental Christmas music, I've drawn a scrolled banner enhanced with fancy flourishes and an attempt at *Olde English* lettering. On it I've written another little line taken from some ancient Yuletide text. Despite the elaborate presentation, the message is a simple one, and I extend it to you and your ukulele for a joyous musical Christmas and a happy musical holiday season:

"At Christmas play and make good cheer, for Christmas comes but once a year."

"Sing choirs of angels, sing in exultation!"

Table of Contents

"Gloria in altissimus Deo, et in terra pax hominibus bonae voluntatis!"

A Child This Day Is Born

Ukulele tuning: gCEA

Traditional

A Child this day is born, a Child of high re - nown, most

worth - y of a sep - ter, a sep - ter and a crown.

Chorus: Now - ell, Now - ell, Now - ell, Now - ell sing all we may, be -

cause the King of all kings was born this bless - ed day.

All Hail To The Days

Ukulele tuning: gCEA

Traditional

1.All hail to the days that mer - it more praise than all the rest of the year,___ and

wel - come the nights that dou - ble de - lights as well for the poor as for peer!___ Good

for - tune at - tend each mer - ry man's friend that doth but the best that he may,___ for -

get - ting old wrongs with car - ols and songs, to drive the cold win - ter a - way.___

All Hail To The Days

2. 'Tis ill for a mind to anger inclined
   To think of small injuries now;
   If wrath be to seek, do not lend her thy cheek,
   Nor let her inhabit thy brow.
   Cross out of thy books malevolent looks,
   Both beauty and youth's decay,
   And wholly consort with mirth and with sport,
   To drive the cold winter away.

3. When Christmas's tide comes in like a bride,
   With holly and ivy clad,
   Twelve days in the year much mirth and good cheer
   In every household is had.
   The country guise is then to devise
   Some gambols of Christmas play,
   Whereat the young men do best that they can
   To drive the cold winter away.

4. This time of the year is spent in good cheer,
   And neighbors together do meet,
   To sit by the fire, with friendly desire,
   Each other in love to greet.
   Old grudges forgot are put in the pot,
   All sorrows aside they lay;
   The old and the young doth carol this song,
   To drive the cold winter away.

Angels We Have Heard On High

Ukulele tuning: gCEA

French-English Traditional

2. Shepherds, why this jubilee?
   Why your joyous strains prolong?
   Say what may the tidings be
   Which inspire your heav'nly song.
   CHORUS

3. Come to Bethlehem and see
   Him whose birth the angels sing.
   Come, adore on bended knee
   Christ, the Lord, the newborn King.
   CHORUS

4. See Him in a manger laid,
   Whom the angels praise above;
   Mary, Joseph, lend your aid,
   While we raise our hearts in love.
   CHORUS

As With Gladness Men Of Old

Ukulele tuning: gCEA

**Words by
WILLIAM DIX**

**Music by
KONRAD KOCHER**

Auld Lang Syne

Ukulele tuning: gCEA

Traditional Scottish

Auld Lang Syne

SCOTTISH LYRICS	TRANSLATION
2. We twa hae run about the braes And pou'd the gowans fine, But we've wander'd monie a weary fit Sin auld lang syne. CHORUS	2. We two have run about the hills And pulled the daisies fine, But we've wandered many a weary foot Since old long ago. CHORUS
3. We twa hae paidl'd in the burn Frae morning sun till dine, But seas between us braid hae roar'd Sin auld lang syne. CHORUS	3. We two have paddled in the stream From morn till dinner time, But seas between us broad have roared Since old long ago. CHORUS
4. And there's a hand my trusty fiere, And gie's a hand o thine, And we'll tak a right guid willie-waught For auld lang syne. CHORUS	4. And there's a hand my trusty friend, And give us a hand of yours, And we will take a right good drink For old long ago. CHORUS

What would New Year's Eve be without "Auld Lang Syne?" It would be like Christmas without "Silent Night" or the dropping of the Times Square ball at midnight without the accompaniment of Guy Lombardo's orchestra and the smooth sounds of its mellow saxophone section. The lyrics, attributed in part to poet Robert Burns, actually stem from an old Scottish folk song. They bring a moment of reflection, a time to look back, a thought of renewing treasured friendships. It is a familiar melody for humming or strumming, for whistling or dancing, one to be played on the parlor piano or whatever instrument is close at hand. But most especially it is a song for the ukulele whose soft chords and steady rhythm provide a perfect background for the nostalgia of the "old long ago."

Away In A Manger

Ukulele tuning: gCEA

Traditional

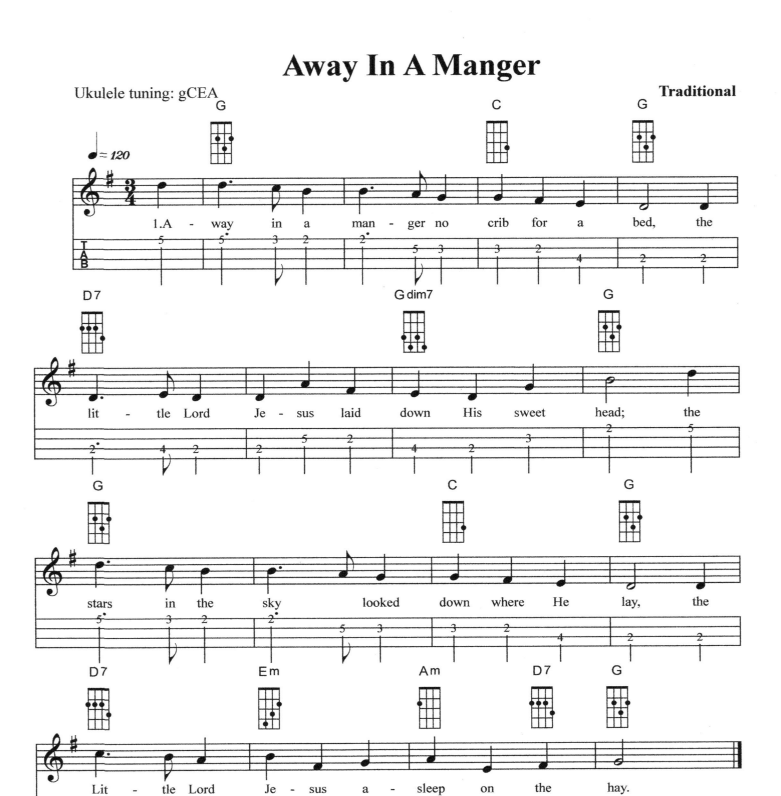

1.A - way in a man - ger no crib for a bed, the
lit - tle Lord Je - sus laid down His sweet head; the
stars in the sky looked down where He lay, the
Lit - tle Lord Je - sus a - sleep on the hay.

2. The cattle are lowing, the poor Baby wakes, but little Lord Jesus no crying He makes;
   I love Thee, Lord Jesus look down from the sky, and stay by my cradle till morning is nigh.

3. Be near me, Lord Jesus, I ask Thee to stay close by me forever and love me I pray;
   Bless all the dear children in Thy tender care, and take me to heaven to live with Thee there.

Away In A Manger
Alternate Version

Traditional

1.A - way in a man - ger no crib for a bed, the
lit - tle Lord Je - sus laid down His sweet head; the
stars in the bright sky looked down where He lay, the
lit - tle Lord Je - sus a - sleep on the hay.

Boar's Head Carol

This is a "macaronic" carol, meaning with words in two languages, English and Latin.
It is a version traditionally sung every Christmas at Queen's College, Oxford, England.

Ukulele tuning: gCEA

Traditional English

2. The boar's head, as I understand,
   Is the rarest dish in all the land,
   Which thus bedecked with a gay garland,
   Let us **servire cantico.**
   CHORUS

3. Our steward hath provided this,
   In honour of the King of bliss,
   Which on this day to be served is,
   In regimensi atrio.
   CHORUS

LATIN TRANSLATION

Quot estis in convivio - So many as are in the feast
Caput apri defero, reddens laudes Domino - The boar's head I bring, giving praises to God
sevire cantico - let us serve with a song
In regimensi atrio -- In the Queen's hall

The Cherry Tree Carol

There are many variants to this old English carol, both in words and music. The origin
of this version is uncertain, but the melody definitely has the feel of an American folk tune.

Ukulele tuning: gCEA

Traditional

1. When Jo - seph was an old man, an old man was he, he

mar - ried Vir - gin Ma - ry, the Queen of Gal - i - lee. He

mar - ried Vir - gin Ma - ry, the Queen of Gal - i - lee.

2. As Joseph and Mary
Walked through an orchard green,
There were apples and cherries
As thick as might be seen.

3. Then Mary spoke to Joseph,
With words meek and mild,
"Joseph, gather me some cherries,
For I am with child," etc.

4. Then Jospeh flew in anger,
In anger flew he,
"Let the father of the baby
Gather cherries for thee," etc.

5. O then besoke Jesus
From the womb words spoke he,
"Let my mother have some cherries,
Bow down then, cherry tree," etc.

6. The cherry tree bow'd down then,
Bow'd down to the ground,
And Mary gathered cherries
While Joseph stood around, etc.

7. As Joseph went a-walking,
He heard angels sing,
"This night there shall be born
Our heavenly King," etc.

Christmas Is Coming

Ukulele tuning: gCEA

Traditional English

Christ-mas is com-ing, the goose is get-ting fat, please to put a pen-ny in the old man's hat.

If you've no pen-ny a ha' pen-ny will do. If you've got no ha' pen-ny then God bless you.

Ha' penny (halfpenny): a small British coin of insignificant value.

A Nursery Rhyme

Little Jack Horner

(Please compose your own melody and ukulele accompaniment.)

Little Jack Horner sat in a corner
Eating his Christmas pie,
He stuck in his thumb and pulled out a plum
And said, "What a good boy am I!"

The Coventry Carol

Ukulele tuning: gCEA

Traditional English

This hauntingly beautiful carol is often mistaken as a lullaby for the Infant Christ Child. In fact, it sadly laments the slaughter of the innocents as depicted in the second chapter of Matthew. Dating back to the 1500s, it was performed in Coventry, England, as part of the mystery play called the Pageant Of The Shearmen And Tailors. The final chord changes the prevailing minor sound to major in what is called a "Picardy third."

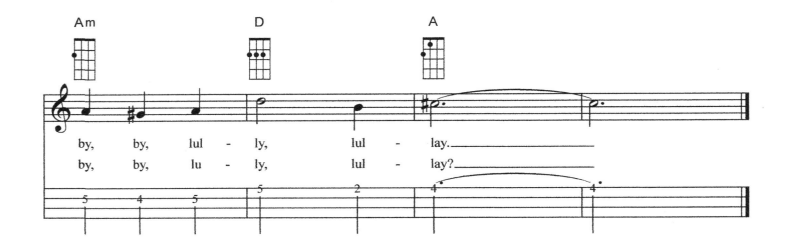

by,   by,   lul - ly,   lul - lay._____

by,   by,   lu - ly,   lul - lay?_____

3. Herod, the king, in his raging,
   Charg-ed he hath this day,
   His men of might, in his own sight,
   All children young to slay.

4. Then woe is me, poor child for thee!
   And ever mourn and say,
   For thy parting nor say nor sing
   By, by, lully lullay.

Deck The Hall

Ukulele tuning: gCEA

Traditional Welsh

1. Deck the hall with boughs of hol - ly, fa la la la la la la la la.
2. See the blaz - ing Yule be - fore us, fa la la la la la la la la.
3. Fast a - way the old year pass - es, fa la la la la la la la la.

'Tis the sea - son to be jol - ly, fa la la la la la la la la.
Strike the harp and join the cho - rus, fa la la la la la la la la.
Hail the new, ye lads and lass - es, fa la la la la la la la la.

Don we now our gay ap - par - el, fa la la la la la la la.
Fol - low me in mer - ry meas - ure, fa la la la la la la la.
Sing we joy - ous all to - geth - er, fa la la la la la la la.

Troll the an - cient Yule - tide car - ol, fa la la la la la la la la.
While I tell of Yule - tide treas - ure, fa la la la la la la la la.
Heed - less of the wind and weath - er, fa la la la la la la la la.

21

The First Nowell

Ukulele tuning: gCEA

Traditional English

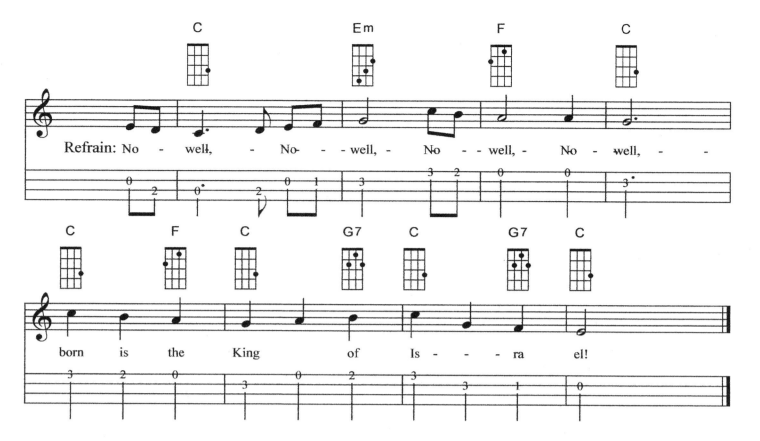

Refrain: No - well, - No- - - well, - No - - well, - No - well, - - born is the King of Is - - ra el!

Because the following three verses relate to the visit of the Magi, this carol is often associated with the Feast of the Epiphany, January 6. This is the "Twelfth Day of Christmas" and is somtimes referred to as Little Christmas. The date is observed by some religious traditions as Christmas Day itself.

2. They looked up and saw a star,
Shining in the east beyond them far,
And to the earth it gave great light,
And so it continued both day and night.
REFRAIN

3. This star drew nigh to the northwest,
O'er Bethlehem it took its rest,
And there it did both stop and stay
Right over the place where Jesus lay.
REFRAIN

4. Then entered in there Wise Men three,
Full rev'rently upon their knee,
And offer'd there in His presence
Their gold and myrrh and frankincense.
REFRAIN

The Friendly Beasts

Ukulele tuning: gCEA

Traditional English

The Friendly Beasts

2. "I", said the donkey, shaggy and brown,
   "I carried His mother up hill and down,
   I carried her safely to Bethlehem town,
   "I", said the donkey, shaggy and brown.

3. "I", said the cow, all white and red,
   "I gave Him my manger for a bed,
   I gave him hay to pillow his head,
   "I", said the cow, all white and red.

4. "I", said the sheep with curly horn,
   "I gave Him my wool for a blanket warm,
   He wore my coat on Christmas morn,
   "I", said the sheep with curly horn.

5. "I", said the dove from the rafters high,
   "I cooed Him to sleep that He should not cry,
   We cooed Him to sleep, my mate and I,
   "I", said the dove from the rafters high.

6. "I", said the camel, yellow and black,
   "Over the desert upon my back,
   I brought Him a gift in the Wise Men's pack,
   "I", said the camel, yellow and black.

7. Thus ev'ry beast by some good spell,
   In the stable dark was glad to tell
   Of the gift he gave Emmanuel,
   The gift he gave Emmanuel.

Gesu Bambino

An Italian Christmas Carol

PIETRO YON

Ukulele tuning: gCEA

Gloucestershire Wassail

Wassail (Wes hal): Old English for "Be thou hale."

Ukulele tuning: gCEA

Ancient English traditional

2. So here is to Cherry and to his right cheek, pray God send our master a good piece of beef,
And a good piece of beef that may we all see, with the wassailing bowl we'll drink to thee.

3. And here is to Dobbin and to his right eye, pray God send our master a good Christmas pie,
A good Christmas pie that may we all see, with our wassailing bowl we'll drink to thee.

4. So here is to Broad May and to her broad horn, may God send our master a good crop of corn,
A good crop of corn that may we all see, with out wassailing bowl we'll drink to thee.

5. And here is to Fillpail and to her left ear, pray God send our master a happy New Year,
A happy New Year as e'er he did see, with our wassailing bowl we'll drink to thee.

6. Then here's to the maid in the lily white smock, who trips to the door and slips back the lock,
Who trips to the door and pulls back the pin, for to let us jolly wassailers in.

Cherry and Dobbin are the names of horses,
Broad May, Fillpail, and Colly are cows.

God Rest You Merry, Gentlemen

Ukulele tuning: gCEA

Traditional English

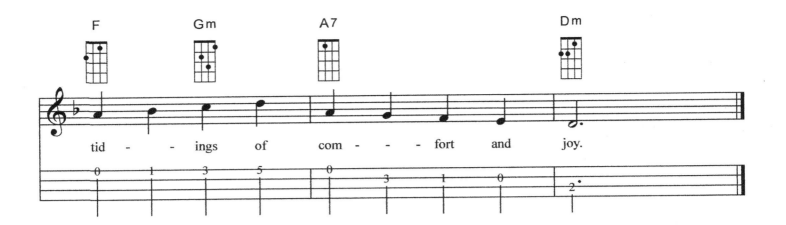

F	Gm	A7	Dm

tid - - ings of com - - - fort and joy.

2. In Bethlehem in Jewry
   This blessed Babe was born,
   And laid within a manger,
   Upon this blessed morn;
   The which His mother Mary
   Did nothing take in scorn.
   CHORUS

3. From God our Heavenly Father
   A blessed angel came,
   And unto certain shepherds
   Brought tidings of the same,
   How that in Bethlehem was born
   The Son of God by name.
   CHORUS

4. The shepherds at those tidings
   Rejoice-ed much in mind,
   And left their flocks a-feeding
   In tempest, storm, and wind,
   And went to Bethlehem straightway,
   The Son of God to find.
   CHORUS

5. But when to Bethlehem they came,
   Whereat this Infant lay,
   They found him in a manger,
   Where oxen feed on hay;
   His mother Mary kneeling,
   Unto the Lord did pray.
   CHORUS

Good Christian Men, Rejoice

Ukulele tuning: gCEA

JOHN NEALE

Traditional German

1.Good Chris - tian men, re - joice with heart and soul and voice;

give ye heed to what we say: News! News! Je - sus Christ is born to - day.

Ox and ass be - fore Him bow, and He is in the man - ger now;

Christ is born to - day! Christ is born to - day!

2. Good Christian men, rejoice
With heart and soul and voice;
Now ye hear of endless bliss:
Joy! Joy!

Jesus Christ was born for this!
He hath ope'd the heav'nly door,
And man is bless-ed evermore;
Christ was born for this!

3 Good Christian men, rejoice
With heart and soul and voice;
Now ye need not fear the grave:
Peace! Peace!
Jesus Christ is born to save!

Calls you one and calls you all
To gain His everlasting hall;
Christ was born to save!
Christ was born to save!

31

Good King Wenceslas

Ukulele tuning: gCEA

Traditional

2. "Hither, Page, and stand by me,
    If thou know'st it, telling.
    Yonder peasant, who is he?
    Where and what his dwelling?"
    "Sire, he lives a good league hence,
    Underneath the mountain,
    Right against the forest fence,
    By St. Agnes' fountain."

3. "Bring me flesh and bring me wine,
    Bring me pine logs hither;
    Thou and I will see him dine,
    When we bear them thither."
    Page and monarch, forth they went,
    Forth they went together
    Through the rude wind's wild lament
    And the bitter weather.

4. "Sire, the night is darker now,
    And the wind blows stronger;
    Fails my heart, I know not how,
    I can go no longer."
    "Mark my footsteps, my good my page,
    Tread thou in them boldly;
    Thou shalt find the winter's rage
    Freeze thy blood less coldly."

5. In his master's steps he trod,
    Where the snow lay dinted;
    Heat was in the very sod
    Which the saint had printed.
    Therefore, Christian men, be sure,
    Wealth or rank possessing,
    Ye who now will bless he poor,
    Shall yourselves find blessing.

Go Tell It On The Mountain

Ukulele tuning: gCEA

American Traditional

1.When I was a seek - er I sought both night and day, I
2.He made me a watch - man, up - on a cit - y wall, and

asked the Lord to help me, and He showed me the way.
if I am a Chris - tian, I am the least of all.

With a swing: Go tell it on the moun - tain, ov - er the hills and ev - 'ry where,

Go tell it on the moun - tain our Je - sus Christ is born.

Hark! The Herald Angels Sing

Ukulele tuning: gCEA

There's an odd twist to this hymn that links it with the printing press invented by Johannes Gutenberg in 1440. Felix Mendelsohn composed a contata in 1870 for an event celebrating the press's invention, and it was this melody that was later fitted to the words Charles Wesley had written many years before. The original hymn was drab and solemn, not the spirited Mendelsohn version we know today. Incidentally, Charles Wesley was the brother of John Wesley, founder of the Methodist church.

Words by
CHARLES WESLEY

Music by
F. MENDELSOHN

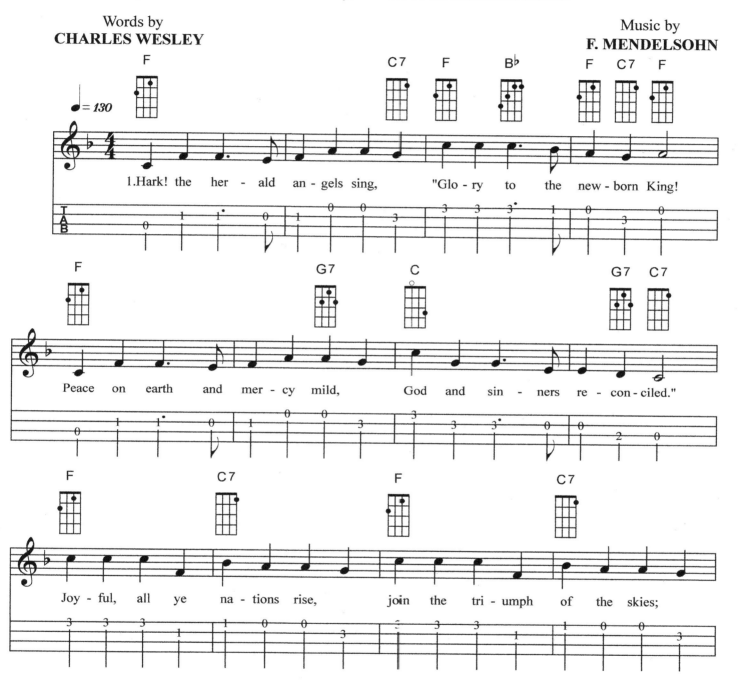

1.Hark! the her - ald an - gels sing, "Glo - ry to the new - born King!

Peace on earth and mer - cy mild, God and sin - ners re - con - ciled."

Joy - ful, all ye na - tions rise, join the tri - umph of the skies;

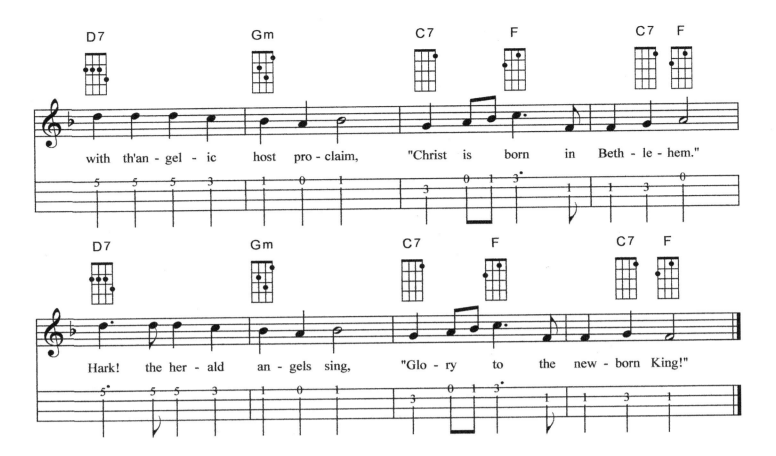

with th'an - gel - ic host pro - claim, "Christ is born in Beth - le - hem."

Hark! the her - ald an - gels sing, "Glo - ry to the new - born King!"

2. Christ, by highest heav'n adored,
   Christ the everlasting Lord;
   Late in time behold Him come,
   Offspring of the virgin's womb.
   Veiled in flesh the Godhead see;
   Hail th'incarnate Deity,
   Pleased on earth with us to dwell,
   Jesus, our Emmanuel!
   Hark! the herald angels sing,
   "Glory to the new-born King."

3. Hail, the heav'n born Prince of Peace!
   Hail, the Son of righteousness!
   Light and life to all He brings,
   Ris'n with healing in His wings.
   Mild He lays His glory by,
   Born that man no more may die,
   Born to raise the sons of earth,
   Born to give them second birth.
   Hark! the herald angels sing,
   "Glory to the newborn King."

Here We Come A-Wassailing

Ukulele tuning: gCEA

Traditional English

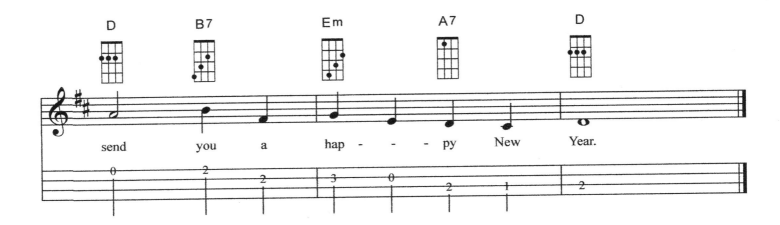

send you a hap - - py New Year.

2. We are not daily beggars
   That beg from door to door,
   But only neighbors' children
   Whom you have seen before:
   CHORUS

3. Our clothes are very ragged,
   Our shoes are very thin,
   We have a little pocket
   To put a penny in:
   CHORUS

4. If you've got no penny
   Then a ha'penny will do,
   And if you've got no ha'penny
   Then God bless you:
   CHORUS

5. Good master and good mistress
   While you're sitting by the fire,
   Pray think of us poor children
   Who are wan'dring in the mire:
   CHORUS

6. God bless the master of this house,
   The mistress bless also,
   And all the little children
   That round the table go:
   CHORUS

7. And all your kin and kinfolk
   That dwell both far and near,
   We wish you a merry Christmas
   And a happy New Year.
   CHORUS

The Holly And The Ivy

Ukulele tuning: gCEA

Traditional

1.The hol - ly and the i - vy, when they are both full grown, of__ all the trees that are in the wood, the__ hol - ly bears the crown.

Chorus: The ris - ing of the sun,____ and the run-ning of the deer, the__ play-ing of the mer - ry or - gan, sweet sing-ing in the choir.

2. The holly bears a prickle, as sharp as any thorn, and Mary bore sweet Jesus Christ on Christmas day in the morn. CHORUS

3. The holly bear a blossom, as white as any flower, and Mary bore sweet Jesus Christ to be our sweet Savior. CHORUS

4. The holly bears a berry, as red as any blood, and Mary bore sweet Jesus Christ to do poor sinners good. CHORUS

The Holly And The Ivy
Alternate Version

Ukulele tuning: gCEA

Traditional English

Oh, the hol - ly and the i - vy are now at last full grown,___ of

all the trees that are in the wood the hol - ly tree bears the crown.

Chorus: Oh, the ris - ing of the sun,___ the run - ing of the deer,___ the

play - ing of the mer - ry or - gan sweet sing - ing all in the choir.___

Huron Carol

Ukulele tuning: gCEA

Original Huron words by Fr. Jean de Brebeuf
English words by Jesse Edgar Middleton

Traditional Canadian
(Old French Melody)

2. Within a lodge of broken bark
   The tender Babe was found,
   A ragged robe of rabbit skin
   Enwrapped His beauty 'round.
   And as the hunter braves drew nigh,
   The angel song ran loud and high:
   REFRAIN

3. The earliest moon of wintertime
   Is not so round and fair,
   As was the ring of glory on
   The helpless Infant there,
   While chiefs from far before Him knelt
   With gifts of fox and beaver pelt.
   REFRAIN

4. O children of the forest free,
   O sons of Manitou,
   The Holy Child of earth and heav'n
   Is born today for you.
   Come, kneel before the radiant Boy
   Who brings you beauty, peace, and joy.
   REFRAIN

Father Jean de Brebeuf, a Jesuit missionary working among the Huron Indians in Canada in the late 1600s, wrote the original lyrics in the Huron language and set them to the tune of an old French folk song. He wanted to tell the Nativity story in a way the Indians could understand and relate to. Some 200 years later, Jesse Middleton, a prolific Canadian author and poet, wrote the beautiful English words that are so rich and vivid in Indian imagery. The hymn is popular in Canada and is considered to be the first Canadian Christmas carol, possibly the first carol written in the New World.

I Heard The Bells On Christmas Day

Ukulele tuning: gCEA

Henry Wadsworth Longfellow (1807-1882) is considered to be one of America's most distinguished poets and certainly the most celebrated poet of his day. Among his many poems are the well-known "Paul Revere's Ride" and "The Song Of Hiawatha." The lyrics of this carol were written as a poem on Christmas Day in 1864 and later set to music by the English organist John Baptiste Calkin. So pronounced is the meter of many of Longfellow's poem that they are musical by themselves.

Words by
HENRY W. LONGFELLOW

Music by
J. BAPTISTE CALKIN

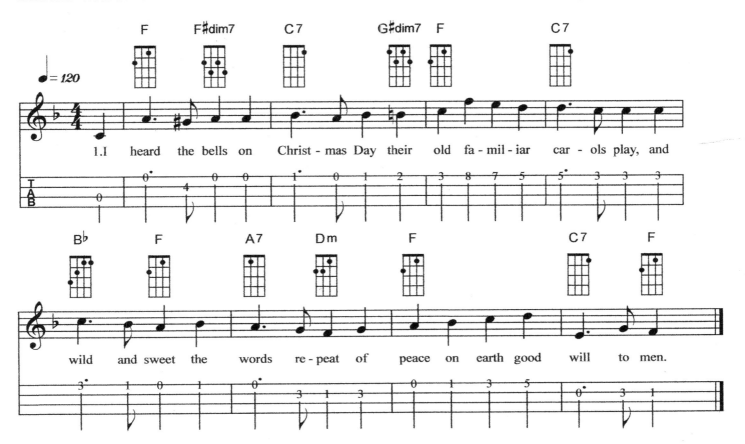

2. I thought how, as the day had come,
   The belfries of all Christendom
   Had rolled along th'unbroken song
   Of peace on earth good will to men.

3. And in despair I bowed my head,
   "There is no peace on earth," I said,
   For hate is strong, and mocks the song
   Of peace on earth good will to men."

4. Then pealed the bells more loud and deep,
   God is not dead, nor doth He sleep,
   The wrong shall fail, the right prevail,
   With peace on earth good will to men.

5. Till, ringing, singing on its way,
   The world revolv'd from night to day,
   A voice, a chime, a chant sublime
   Of peace on earth good will to men.

In The Bleak Midwinter

Ukulele tuning: gCEA

Words by
Christina Rossetti

Music by
Gustav Holst

2. Our God, heav'n cannot hold Him,
Nor earth sustain;
Heav'n and earth shall flee away
When He comes to reign.
In the bleak midwinter
A stable place sufficed,
The Lord God incarnate,
Jesus Christ.

3. Enough for Him, whom cherubim
Worship night and day,
A breast full of milk
And manger full of hay.
Enough for Him whom angels
Fall down before,
Ox and ass and camel
Which adore.

4. Angels and archangels
May have gathered there,
Cherubim and seraphim
Throng-ed the air;
But His mother only,
In her maiden bliss,
Worshiped the Beloved
With a kiss.

5. What can I give Him,
Poor as I am?
If I were a shepherd,
I would bring a lamb;
If I were a Wise Man,
I would do my part;
Yet what I can I give Him
Give my heart.

These lyrics were originally written as a Christmas poem by the English poet Christine Rossetti. The poem was published posthumously and later set to music by Gustav Holts, an English composer. Its inclusion in "The English Hymnal" in 1906 gave rise to its popularity as a Christmas carol. Holts is renown for his orchestral work "The Planets" and for the beautiful melodies of his compositions. How evident this is in the skillful match of music to Rossetti's picturesque words.

I Saw Three Ships

Ukulele tuning: gCEA

Traditional English

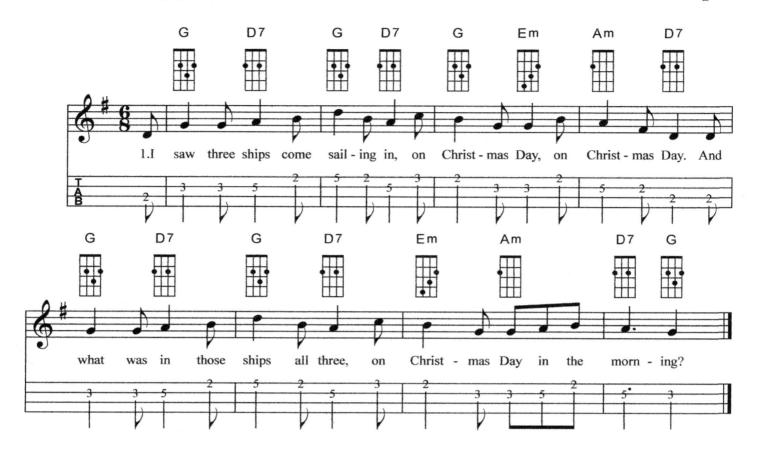

2. Our Savior Christ and His lady,
   On Christmas Day, on Christmas Day,
   Our Savior Christ and His lady,
   On Christmas Day in the morning.

3. Pray, wither sailed those ships all three?
   On Christmas Day, on Christmas Day,
   Pray, wither sailed those ships all three?
   On Christmas Day in the morning.

4. O, they sailed into Bethlehem, etc.

5. And all the bells on earth shall ring, etc.

6. And all the angels in heaven shall sing, etc.

7. And all the souls on earth shall sing, etc.

8. Then let us all rejoice, amen, etc.

It Came Upon The Midnight Clear

Ukulele tuning: gCEA

Words by
EDMOND H. SEARS

Music by
RICHARD S. WILLIS

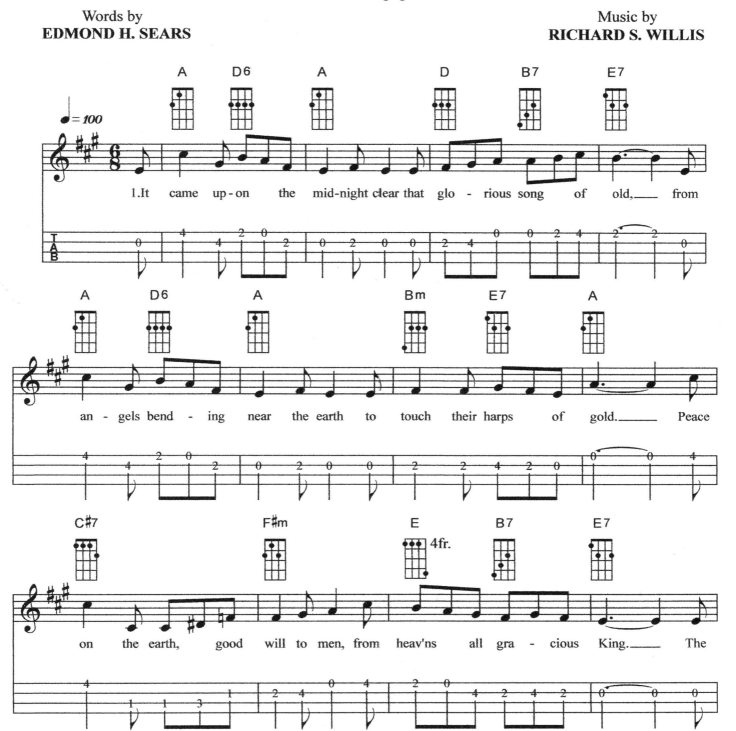

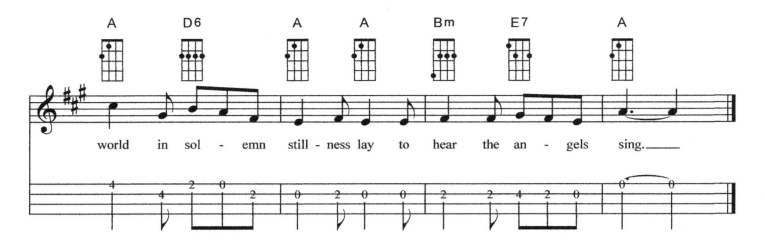

world   in   sol - emn   still - ness lay   to   hear   the   an - gels   sing._____

2. Still thro' the cloven skies they came,
   With graceful wings unfurl'd,
   And still their heav'nly music floats
   O'er all the weary world.
   Above its sad and lowly plains
   They bend on hov'ring wing,
   And ever o'er its Babel sounds
   The blessed angels sing.

3. O ye, beneath life's crushing load,
   Whose forms are bending low,
   Who toil along the climbing way
   With painful steps and slow,
   Look now, for glad and golden hours
   Come swiftly on the wing,
   O rest beside the weary road
   And hear the angels sing.

4. For lo! the days are hast'ning on,
   By prophets seen of old,
   When with the ever circling years,
   Shall come the time foretold,
   When the new heav'n and earth shall own
   The Prince of Peace their King,
   And the whole world send back the song
   Which now the angels sing.

Jingle Bells

Ukulele tuning: gCEA

Traditional

1.Dash - ing through the snow, in a one-horse o - pen sleigh,

o'er the fields we go, laugh - ing all the way.

Bells on Bob - tail ring, mak - ing spir - its bright, what

fun it is to ride and sing a sleigh - ing song to - night.

Jingle Bells

2. A day or two ago, I thought I'd take a ride, and soon Miss Fannie Bright was seated by my side.
The horse was lean and lank, misfortune seem'd his lot, he got into a drifted bank and then we got upsot!
CHORUS

3. Now the ground is white, go it while you're young, take the girls tonight and sing this sleighing song.
Just get a bobtail'd bay, two-forty for his speed, hitch him to an open sleigh, and crack! you'll take the lead.
CHORUS

Joy To The World

Ukulele tuning: gCEA

Isaac Watts (1674-1748) is considered to be England's foremost writer of hymns, with more than 700 attributed to him, many of which are still sung today. George Frideric Handel, the celebrated classical composer, German born but English naturalized, was a contemporary of Watts. Despite common belief, he did not write the entire music for this hymn. It does however contain several adaptations drawn from his works including the "Messiah." "Joy To The World" is claimed to be the most most popular of all Christmas hymns.

Words by
ISAAC WATTS

Music by
GEORGE F. HANDEL

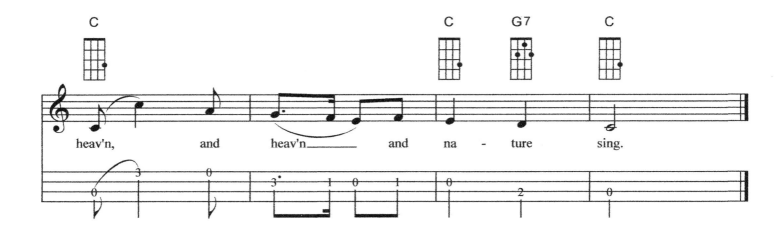

heav'n,   and   heav'n_____ and na - ture sing.

2. Joy to the earth! The Saviour reigns.
   Let men their songs employ.
   While fields and floods, rocks, hills, and plains
   Repeat the sounding joy,
   Repeat the sounding joy,
   Repeat, repeat the sounding joy.

3. No more let sins and sorrows grow,
   Nor thorns infest the grounds.
   He comes to make His blessings flow
   Far as the curse is found,
   Far as the curse is found,
   Far as, far as the curse is found.

4. He rules the world with truth and grace,
   And makes the nations prove
   The glories of His righteousness,
   And wonders of His love,
   And wonders of His love,
   And wonders, and wonders of His love.

Lo, How A Rose E'er Blooming

Ukulele tuning: gCEA

Masters In This Hall

Ukulele tuning: gCEA

Words by
WILLIAM MORRIS

Traditional French

1.Mas - ters in this hall, _____ hear ye news to - day _____

Brought from o - ver sea, _____ and ev - er I you pray.

Chorus: Now - ell! Now - ell! Now - ell! Now - ell sing we clear! Holp - en

are all folk on earth, _____ born _____ is God's Son so dear.

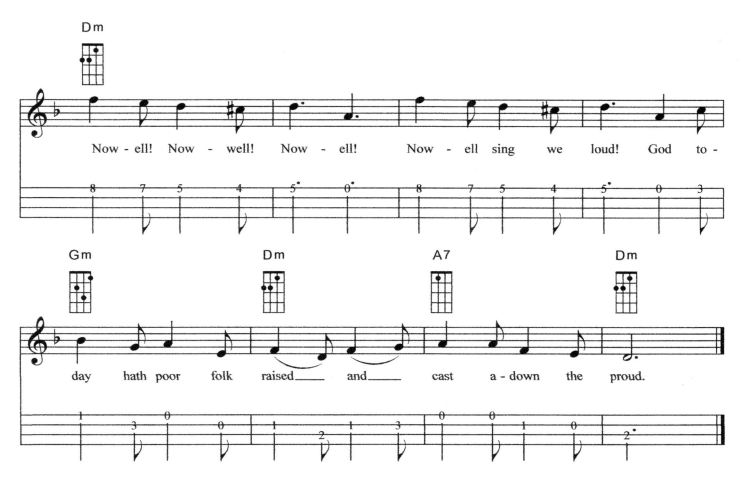

Dm

Now - ell! Now - well! Now - ell! Now - ell sing we loud! God to -

Gm   **Dm**   **A7**   **Dm**

day hath poor folk raised____ and____ cast a - down the proud.

2. "How name ye this Lord,
Shepherds?" then said I.
"Very God," they said,
"Come from heaven high."
CHORUS

3. Ox and ass Him know,
Kneeling on their knee,
Wondrous joy had I
This little Babe to see.
CHORUS

4. This is Christ the Lord,
Masters, be ye glad!
Christmas is come in,
And no folk should be sad.
CHORUS

Noël Nouvelet

The words to this carol written in Old French tell the Christmas story of the Holy Family in Bethleham,
the stable birth of Jesus, the angel appearing to the shepherds, and the three Wise Men bearing their gifts.

Ukulele tuning: gCEA

Ancient French

O Christmas Tree

Ukulele tuning: gCEA

Traditional German

2. O Christmas tree, O Christmas tree,
   Much pleasure thou can'st give me;
   How often has the Christmas tree,
   Afforded me the greatest glee.
   O Christmas tree, O Christmas tree,
   Much pleasure thou can'st give me.

3. O Christmas tree, O Christmas tree,
   Thy candles shine so brightly.
   From base to summit gay and bright,
   There's always splendor for the sight.
   O Christmas tree, O Christmas tree,
   Thy candles shine so brightly.

4. O Christmas tree, O Christmas tree,
   How richly God has decked thee.
   Thou bidst us true and faithful be,
   And trust inGod unchangingly,
   O Christmas tree, O Christmas tree,
   How richly God has decked thee.

O Tannenbaum, O Tannenbaum,
Wie grun sind deine Blatter.
Du grunst nicht nur zur Sommerzeit,
Nein, auch im Winter, wenn es scheit.
O Tannenbaum, O Tannenbaum,
Wie grun sind deine Blatter.

O Come, All Ye Faithful

Ukulele tuning: gCEA

Traditional

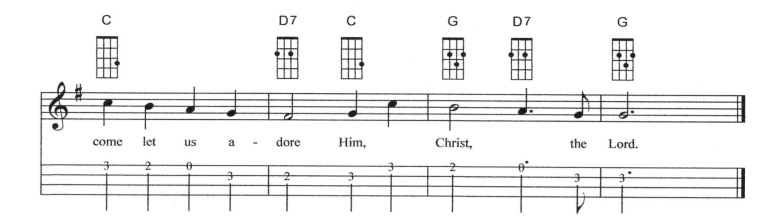

come let us a - dore Him, Christ, the Lord.

2. Sing, choirs of angels,
   Sing in exultation;
   Sing, all ye citizens of heav'n above;
   Glory to God in the highest;
   REFRAIN

3. Yea, Lord, we greet Thee,
   Born this happy morning;
   Jesus to Thee be glory giv'n,
   Word of the Father now in flesh appearing;
   REFRAIN

LATIN LYRICS

Adeste, fideles, laeti, triumphantes;
Venite, venite in Bethlehem.
Natum videte
Regem angelorum.
Venite, adoremus,
Venite, adoremus,
Venite, adoremus Dominum.

Deum de Deo, Lumen de Lumine,
Gestant puellae viscera,
Deum verum,
Genitum, non factum.
Venite, adoremus,
Venite, adoremus,
Venite, adoremus Dominum,

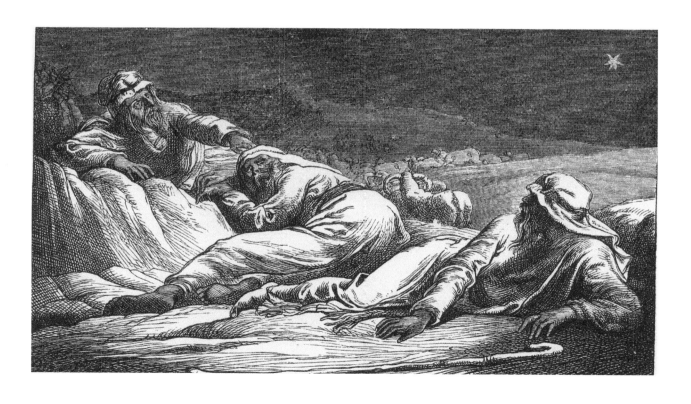

O Little Town of Bethlehem

Ukulele tuning: gCEA

Traditional

O Little Town of Bethlehem

2. For Christ is born of Mary;
   And, gathered all above,
   While mortals sleep, the angels keep
   Their watch of wond'ring love.
   O morning stars, together
   Proclaim the holy birth;
   And praises sing to God the King,
   And peace to men on earth.

3. O holy child of Bethlehem,
   Descend to us, we pray;
   Cast out our sin, and enter in,
   Be born to us today.
   We hear the Christmas angels
   The great glad tidings tell;
   O come to us, abide with us,
   Our Lord Emmanuel.

4. How silently, how silently,
   The wondrous gift is given!
   So God imparts to human hearts
   The blessing of His heaven.
   No ear may hear His coming,
   But in this world of sin,
   Where meek souls will receive Him, still
   The dear Christ enters in.

Once In Royal David's City

Ukulele tuning: gCEA

Traditional

3. Jesus is our childhood's pattern,
   Day by day like us He grew;
   He was little, weak, and helpless,
   Tears and smiles like us He knew;
   For He feeleth for our sadness,
   And He shareth in our gladness.

4. And our eyes at last shall see Him,
   Through His own redeeming love.
   For that Child so dear and gentle
   Is our Lord in heav'n above;
   And He leads His children on
   To the place where He is gone.

O Thou Joyful Day

Ukulele tuning: gCEA

Taditional Sicilian

O thou joy - ful day, O thou bless - ed day,

glad - some peace - ful Christ - mas - tide.

1. Earth's hopes a - wak en, Christ life has tak - en,
2. Christ's life is beam - ing, our souls re - deem - ing,
3. King of all glo - ry, we bow be - fore Thee,

Praise Him, O praise Him on ev - 'ry side.

Past Three O'Clock

In olden times, night watchmen called Waifs would patrol the dark streets carrying their lanterns and calling out the hours, the weather, and a comforting "All is well!" This traditional refrain, sometimes referred to as "London Waits," traces its history back to the Renaissance days of the 1600s. Since then many variations of melody have occurred and numerous Christmas verses have been added. Brief as it is, it only seems right that this snippet of a refrain with its long association to Christmas should stand by itself and be considered something of a carol in its own right.

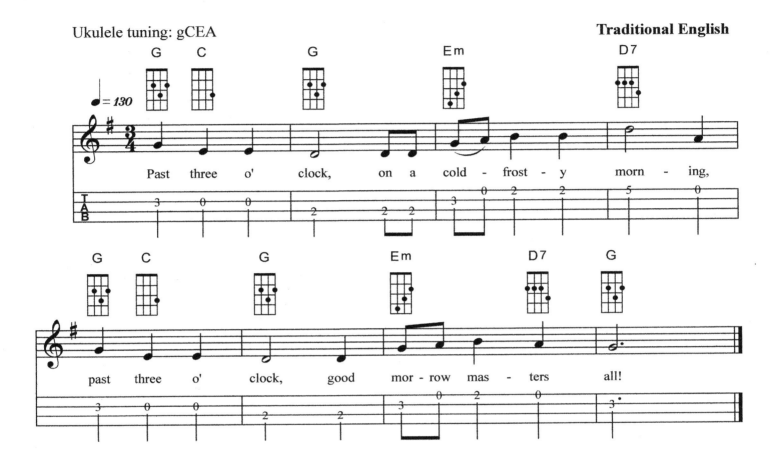

A Nursery Rhyme
Little Jack Horner
(Please compose your own melody and ukulele accompaniment.)

Little Jack Horner sat in a corner
Eating his Christmas pie,
He stuck in his thumb and pulled out a plum
And said, "What a good boy am I!"

Silent Night

Ukulele tuning: gCEA

This beloved carol known around the world was first performed in 1818 at Midnight Mass on Christmas Eve in the village church of St. Nicholas in Oberndorf, Austria. Joseph Mohr, an assistant parish priest, wrote the words two years earlier, then gave them to choir master Franz Gruber to make an arrangement for the guitar. Perhaps this was because the church organ was not functioning or because Fr. Moh wished to play the song on the guitar himself. The earliest manuscript indicates that the carol was written in the key of D. Unfortunately that key does not comfortably fit the range of the ukulele.

Words by
JOSEPH MOHR

Music by
FRANZ GRUBER

2. Silent night, holy night,
   Shepherds quake at the sight.
   Glories stream from heaven afar,
   Heavenly hosts sing "Alleluia!"
   Christ, the Saviour, is born,
   Christ, the Saviour, is born.

3. Silent night, holy night,
   Son of God, love's pure light.
   Radiant beams from Thy holy face,
   With the dawn of redeeming grace.
   Jesus, Lord, at Thy birth,
   Jesus, Lord, as Thy birth.

4. Stille Nacht, heilige Nacht!
   Alles schlaft, einsam wacht;
   Nur das traute hochheilige Paar.
   Holder Knabe im lockigen Haar,
   Schlaf in himmlisher Ruh,
   Schlaf in himmilsher Ruh.

The Snow Lay On The Ground

Ukulele tuning: gCEA

Traditional

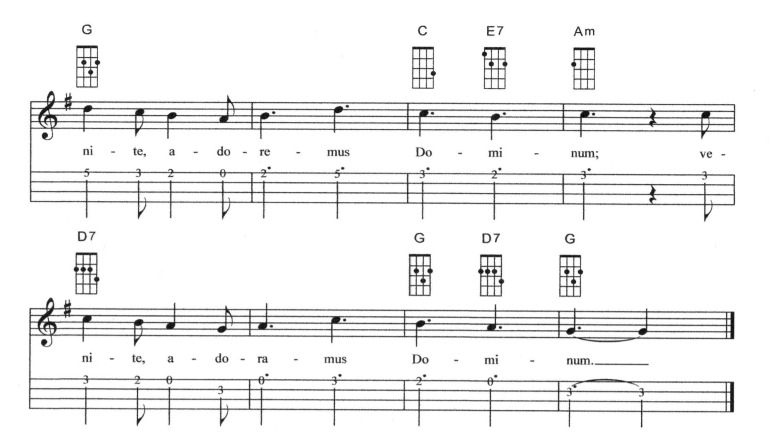

2. 'Twas Mary, daughter pure, came to the creche,
   And brought into this world the Word made flesh.
   She laid Him in a stall at Bethlehem;
   The ass and oxen shared the roof with them.
   Venite, adoremus ... etc.

3. Saint Joseph, too, was near to tend the Child,
   To guard Him and protect His mother mild.
   The angels hover'd 'round, and sang this song:
   Venite, adoremus Dominum.
   Venite, adoremus ... etc.

4. And thus that manger poor became a throne,
   For He whom Mary bore was God the Son.
   O come, then, let us join the heav'nly host,
   To praise the Father, Son, and Holy Ghost.
   Venite, adoremus ... etc.

SUSSEX CAROL

Ukulele tuning: gCEA

Traditional English

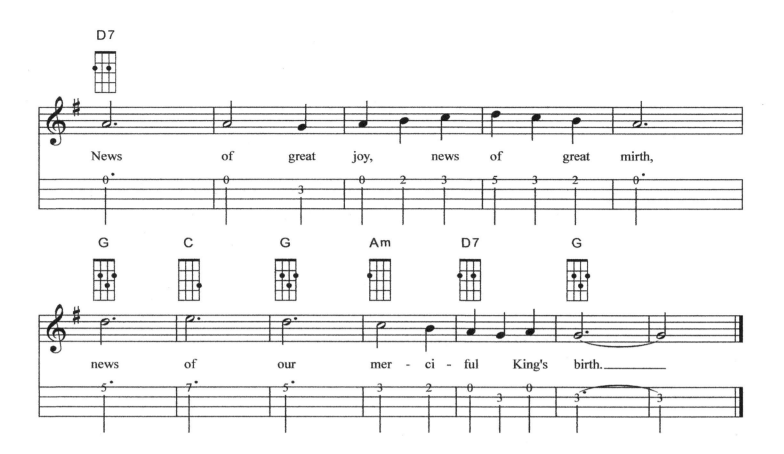

News of great joy, news of great mirth,

news of our mer - ci - ful King's birth._____

2. When sin departs before Thy grace,
   Then life and health come in its place.
   When sin departs before Thy grace,
   Then life and health come in its place.
   Angels and men with joy may sing,
   All for to see the newborn King.

3. All out of darkness we have light,
   Which made the angels sing this night.
   All out of darkness we have light,
   Which made the angels sing this night.
   "Glory to God and peace to men,
   Now and forever more. Amen."

Sweet Chiming Bells

Ukulele tuning: gCEA

This delightful carol comes from a Yorkshire pub singing tradition and is said to be one of many variants for "While Shepherds Watched." The words of the verses are from a poem by Clara Broughton Conant entitled "A Song For Christmas Eve." They were substituted by the group Nowell Sing We Clear as recorded on their album "Come, Smiling Morn!" Permission for use has been kindly granted. Thanks too to Tony Barrand and John Roberts of Nowell Sing We Clear for the alternate version of "The Holly And The Ivy" also included in this collection.

CLARA BROUGHTON CONANT   **Traditional English**

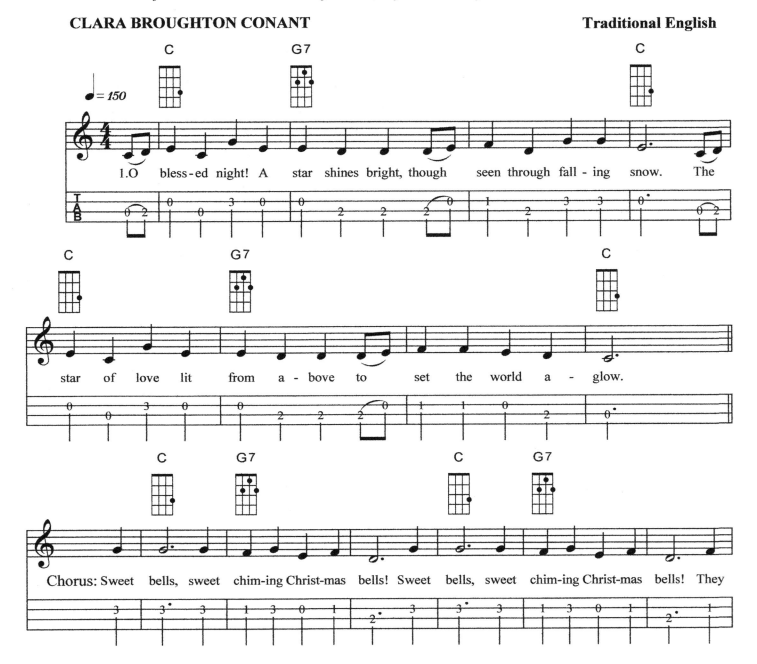

Sweet Chiming Bells

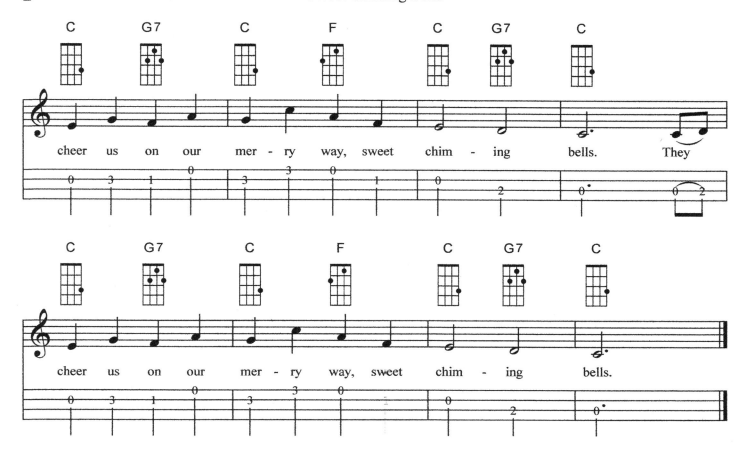

2. Child voices sweet once more repeat the angels' glorious strain;
   Our gray old Earth, in holy mirth, becomes a child again.
   CHORUS

3. Chime sweetly on, ye Christmas bells, while happy voices sing;
   Shine out, O star, from heaven afar and guide us to our King.
   CHORUS

4. To hail the little new-born King, a few poor shepherds came,
   Although with wonder, joy, and love the heavens were aflame.
   CHORUS

5. The wise men came upon their way, led by that heavenly light;
   O, star of love, shine from above and make our pathway bright.
   CHORUS

6. The loving heart, the prayer of faith, are sweeter gifts to bring;
   Shine out, O star, from heaven afar and guide us to our King.
   CHORUS

We Three Kings Of Orient Are

Ukulele tuning: gCEA

Traditional

1.We three kings of O - ri - ent are; bear - ing gifts we trav - erse a - far,
2.Born a King on Beth - le - hem's plain. Gold I bring to crown Him a - gain.

field and foun - tain, moor and moun - tain, fol - low - ing yon - der star.
King for - ev - er, ceas - ing nev - er, o - ver us all to reign.

Refrain: O____ Star of won - der, star of night, star of roy - al beau - ty bright.

West - ward lead - ing, still pro - ceed - ing, guide us to Thy per - fect light.

2. Born a King on Bethlehem's plain.
Gold I bring to crown Him again.
King forever, ceasing never,
Over us all to reign.
REFRAIN

3. Frankincense to offer have I,
Incense owns a Deity nigh.
Pray'r and praising, all men raising,
Worship Him God most high.
REFRAIN

4. Myrrh is mine, its bitter perfume
Breathes a life of gathering gloom;
Sorrowing, sighing, bleeding, dying,
Sealed in the stone-cold tomb.
REFRAIN

5. Glorious now behold Him arise, King and God and sacrifice, Alleluia, alleluia, Earth to heav'n replies. REFRAIN

What Child Is This?

Ukulele tuning: gCEA

Traditional English

1.What Child is this, who laid to rest on Ma - ry's lap is sleep - ing? Whom

an - gels greet with an - thems sweet, while shep - herds watch are keep - ing?

this is the King, whom shep - herds guard and an - gels sing.

Haste, haste to bring Him laud the Babe, the Son of Ma - ry!

What Child Is This?

2. Why lies He in such mean estate,
   Where ox and ass are feeding?
   Good Christian, fear; for sinners here
   The silent word is pleading.
   Nails, spear shall pierce Him through,
   The cross be borne for me, for you,
   Hail, hail, the Word made flesh,
   The Babe, the Son of Mary!

3. So bring Him incense, gold, and myrrh,
   Come peasant, king, to own Him;
   The King of kings, salvation brings,
   Let loving hearts enthrone Him.
   Raise, raise, the song on high,
   The Virgin sings her lullaby,
   Joy, joy, for Christ is born,
   The Babe, the Son of Mary!

ADDITIONAL NEW YEAR VERSES

1. The old year now away is fled,
   The new year it is en-ter-ed,
   Then let us now our sins downtread,
   And joyfully all appear.
   Let's merry be this day,
   And let us now both sport and play,
   Hang grief, cast care away,
   God send us a happy New Year.

2. And now with New Year's gifts each friend
   Unto each other they do send;
   God grant we may all our lives amend,
   And that the truth may appear.
   Now, like the snake, your skin
   Cast off of evil thoughts and sin,
   And so the year begin,
   God send us a happy New Year.

Note: The melody of this carol is the same as the Elizabethan folk song "Greensleeves."
Like "The Coventry Carol" it ends on a major chord called a Pickardy Third.

While Shepherds Watched Their Flocks

Ukulele tuning: gCEA

Traditional

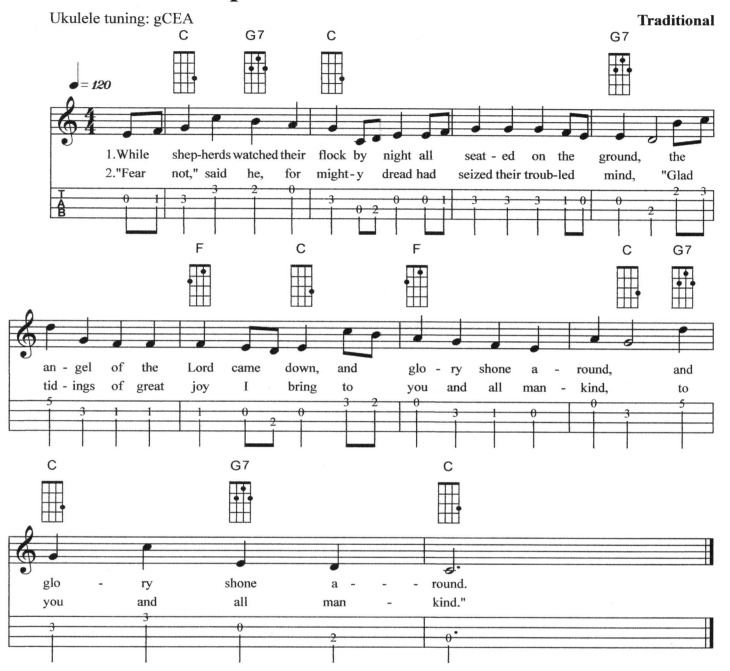

3. "To you in David's town this day
   Is born of David's line,
   The Savior who is Christ the Lord,
   And this shall be His sign,
   And this shall be His sign."

4. "The heav'nly Babe you there shall find,
   To human view displayed,
   All meanly wrapped in swathing bands,
   And in a manger laid,
   And in a manger laid."

5. Thus spake the seraph, and forthwith
   Appeared a shining throng
   Of angels praising God, who thus
   Addressed their joyful song:

6. "All glory be to God on high,
   And to the earth be peace;
   Good-will henceforth from heav'n to men
   Begin and never cease,
   Begin and never cease."

Winds Through The Olive Trees

Ukulele tuning: gCEA

Traditional

We Wish You A Merry Christmas

Ukulele tuning: gCEA

Traditional English

Wexford Carol

Ukulele tuning: gCEA

Traditional Irish

Wexford Carol

2. The night before that happy tide,
   The noble Virgin and her guide,
   Were long time seeking up and down
   To find a lodging in the town.
   But mark how all things come to pass:
   From ev'ry door, repell'd, alas!
   As long foretold, their refuge all
   Was but an humble ox's stall.

3. Near Bethlehem did shepherds keep
   Their flocks of lambs and feeding sheep;
   To whom God's angels did appear,
   Which put the shepherds in great fear;
   "Prepare and go," the angels said,
   "To Bethlehem, be not afraid;
   For there you'll find, this happy morn,
   A princely babe, sweet Jesus born."

4. With thankful heart and joyful mind,
   The shepherds went the babe to find.
   And as God's angel had foretold,
   They did our Saviour Christ behold.
   Within a manger He was laid,
   And by His side the virgin maid,
   Attending on the Lord of life,
   Who came on earth to end all strife.

5. There were three wise men from afar
   Directed by a glorious star,
   And on they wandered night and day
   Until they came where Jesus lay.
   And when they came unto that place
   Where our beloved Messiah was,
   They humbly cast them at His feet,
   With gifts of gold and incense sweet.

The first thing I heard that Christmas morning when I turned on the radio was the soft voice of a woman singing this lovely Celtic carol "a capella." The melody stayed with me all that day, then on through the holidays. It continues even now. The F natural in the melody and accompanying F chord are what distinguish this haunting piece, as well as the B-flat notes and Gm chord. Timing of the third line is challenging but well worth the effort.

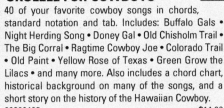